ISAAC ASIMOV'S
Pioneers of Science and Exploration

CHRISTOPHER COLUMBUS

Navigator to the New World

by Isaac Asimov

Gareth Stevens Children's Books
MILWAUKEE

For a free color catalog describing Gareth Stevens' list of high-quality children's books, call 1-800-341-3569 (USA) or 1-800-461-9120 (Canada).

Picture Credits

Mary Evans Picture Library — 8, 12, 13, 29, 36, 43; Courtesy of the Hispanic Society of America, New York — 10-11; The National Maritime Museum, London — 34, 35, 37; U.S. Virgin Islands Division of Tourism — 33.

Library of Congress Cataloging-in-Publication Data

Asimov, Isaac, 1920-
    Christopher Columbus, navigator to the new world / by Isaac Asimov. — "A Gareth Stevens Children's Books ed."
       p. cm. — (Isaac Asimov's pioneers of exploration)
    Includes bibliographical references and index.
    Summary: Describes the life of Columbus as a young man, and as an explorer who marshalled the best technology of his time to explore new lands.
    ISBN 0-8368-0556-9
    1. Columbus, Christopher—Juvenile literature. 2. Explorers—America—Biography—Juvenile literature. 3. Explorers—Spain—Biography—Juvenile literature. 4. America—Discovery and exploration—Spanish—Juvenile literature. [1. Columbus, Christopher. 2. Explorers. 3. America—Discovery and exploration—Spanish.] I. Title. II. Series: Asimov, Isaac, 1920-   Isaac Asimov's pioneers of exploration.
E111.A84   1991
970.01'5—dc20   [B]   [92]   90-25836

A Gareth Stevens Children's Books edition

Edited, designed, and produced by
Gareth Stevens Children's Books
1555 North RiverCenter Drive, Suite 201
Milwaukee, Wisconsin 53212, USA

Series editors: Elizabeth Kaplan and Amy Bauman
Editorial assistant: Scott Enk
Series designer: Kristi Ludwig
Picture researcher: Daniel Helminak
Assistant picture researcher: Diane Laska
Illustrator: Tom Redman

Printed in the United States of America

 2 3 4 5 6 7 8 9 95 94 93

CONTENTS

IN THE MIDDLE OF THE ATLANTIC

Three ships were crossing the Atlantic Ocean, heading west. They were small ships, not made for sailing on the open ocean. Many of the men on board the ships didn't want to be there. Some of them had been prisoners and had only signed up for the voyage to get out of jail.

Many of the crew members didn't like the captain. They were Spaniards, and he was an Italian. Worse yet, many of them thought he was crazy because he believed that by sailing west, he could get to the East. He was sure they could cross the Atlantic Ocean and reach the Orient — the rich lands of India, China, and Japan.

For the crew, the journey was taking too long. Strong winds pushed them west, and they didn't think they'd ever be able to sail back home to Spain. They demanded that the captain turn around. But the captain faced them down. He told them that they would never get back to Spain without him. So the ships sailed on, and eventually, they *did* reach land.

The captain was Christopher Columbus. The year was 1492. In the autumn of that year, Columbus and his crew landed on islands they thought lay along the coast of Asia. In time, however, people realized that Columbus and his crew had found their way to a new world. Because of this man, history was changed.

FROM GENOA TO PORTUGAL

Large wooden ships with sails billowing in the breeze made their way out of the harbor. Merchants and sailors bumped elbows along the crowded docks. The salty smell of the sea floated through back alleys to all parts of Genoa. It was in this Italian port city that Christopher Columbus was born in 1451.

Columbus's father was a weaver and a wine merchant. Going on trading missions for his father may have given Columbus his first experience at sea. He may have sailed to other coastal Italian cities to sell his father's wool cloth and pick up casks of wine. In his early twenties, he probably crossed the Mediterranean Sea on various merchant ships.

When Columbus was twenty-five, he was hired onto a ship headed for ports on the Atlantic Ocean. Off the coast of Portugal, his ship was attacked. When it was clear that the ship would be destroyed, Columbus threw himself into the sea. With an oar to keep himself afloat, he swam 6 miles (10 km) to the Portuguese coast.

In the late 1400s, Portugal was the seafaring capital of Europe. In the early 1400s, the Portuguese prince Henry (who came to be called "the Navigator") started a school for sailors and mapmakers at the southern tip of Portugal. Henry invited Europe's most gifted geographers, most talented shipbuilders, and most experienced sea captains to teach at the school. These people passed their knowledge

Prince Henry of Portugal (1394-1460) had a tremendous effect on many of the early explorers, including Columbus.

to the Portuguese sailors. By Christopher Columbus's day, Portugal was the best place to learn navigation.

And Columbus was more than ready to improve his sailing skills. Over the next

few years, while living in Portugal, he learned to plan out routes on maps and to navigate by compass. He learned to pack provisions for difficult voyages. He gained experience bartering with non-Europeans who didn't speak his language. He learned how to read and write so he would be able to keep records on long voyages.

By 1484, Columbus had risen in rank from a common sailor to the commander of a ship. Even more important, he started to dream of making explorations of his own.

As a young sailor, Christopher Columbus took part in a battle that destroyed the ship on which he was sailing. Columbus swam several miles to shore despite a wound.

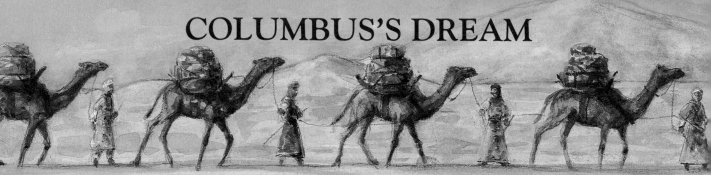

COLUMBUS'S DREAM

Columbus's dreams focused on one place — the Orient. Spices, silks, gold, and jewels all came from the faraway lands of Japan, China, and India. Europeans craved these goods, but getting them was not easy. Arabs and Turks controlled the long caravan routes across the vast plains and deserts of Asia. They charged very high prices for the goods they transported.

The Portuguese, inspired by Henry the Navigator, had begun searching for a sea route to India. By the early 1480s, Portuguese explorers were inching their way down the west coast of Africa, searching for a passageway to the Indian Ocean. They had confidence that they could find another way to the Orient.

Columbus, however, had another idea. He thought he could find a shortcut to the Orient by sailing straight west. Like most educated people of his day, Columbus realized that the earth was round. But no one knew exactly how big around the earth was.

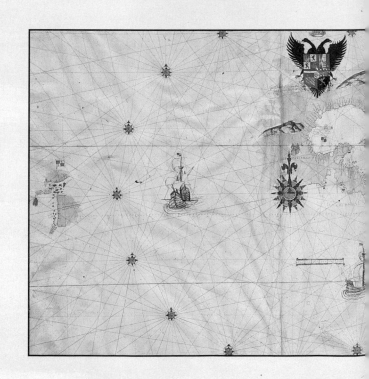

This map shows the world as it was thought to look in the early centuries of exploration. This map was created in 1526.

For centuries, difficult overland routes were the only means of obtaining the spices of the Orient. Through the work of explorers such as Columbus, sea routes to the East became possible.

To answer that question, Columbus wrote to Europe's best-known geographer, Paolo del Pozzo Toscanelli. Toscanelli wrote back, saying that, according to his figures, the earth was 18,000 miles (28,800 km) around.

Toscanelli also estimated that the group of islands now known as Japan was only 3,000 miles (4,800 km) from the coast of Europe.

That was all the proof that Columbus needed. He was sure he could manage the trip.

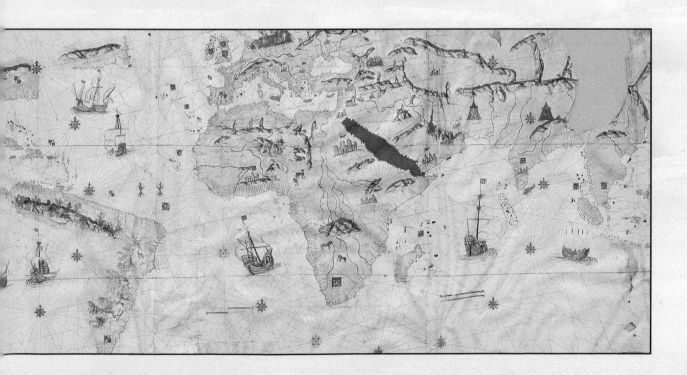

Left: King John II of Portugal refused to support Columbus's expedition.

After all, the distance was shorter than the 11,000 miles (17,600 km) that the Portuguese were willing to travel going around the coast of Africa to India.

In 1484, Columbus went to the king of Portugal, John II, with his idea. King John turned the matter over to his navigators. The Portuguese navigators just shook their heads. They were convinced that the earth was larger around than 18,000 miles (28,800 km).

And even if Columbus's information about the earth's size was correct, they doubted he could make the 3,000-mile (4,800-km) trip. He would have to cross the distance over open sea without the aid of charts or maps. They were sure that on such a voyage, Columbus would get lost and never be heard from again. The Portuguese route to the Orient might be longer, they reasoned, but the ships traveled mainly along the African coast. They could land at trading posts, pick up supplies, and travel by easy stages. King John politely but firmly turned Columbus down.

Columbus next turned to King Ferdinand and Queen Isabella of Spain. The Spanish monarchs were interested in

Queen Isabella and King Ferdinand of Spain. In 1485, Columbus traveled to Spain to meet with the king and queen and to persuade them to finance his trip to the Orient.

Columbus's plan. They were jealous of the Portuguese and their progress in finding a new route to the Orient. They wanted to find their own route to these rich lands. But Spain was in no shape to sponsor Columbus's voyage. The country was in the middle of a costly war to drive the Moors (a group of Muslims who had ruled Spain for centuries) from the country. Columbus's plan would have to wait.

But patience was not one of Columbus's strengths. He was sure that his plan was a good one, but he needed people to listen to it. From 1486 to 1492, Columbus pleaded with Ferdinand and Isabella to sponsor his expedition. Each time they met, the king and queen considered Columbus's plan, but each time, they also put him off.

And each time they met, Columbus made greater demands. First, he only wanted Spain to pay for his voyage. Later, he wanted to be named governor of any new lands he discovered. Next, he insisted that the governorship should be a hereditary position. In the end, he wanted Spain to pay him and his heirs a percentage of any money the country made from his discoveries. With such high demands, Ferdinand and Isabella turned Columbus down even after the war with the Moors was over in 1492.

On hearing about this final rejection, a court adviser begged the king and queen to reconsider. Columbus's demands were small compared with the riches Spain would gain if he were successful. Just a day after Ferdinand and Isabella sent Columbus away, they called him back. This time, they agreed to all of Columbus's demands. Columbus began preparing for his long-awaited adventure.

3

ONWARD TO THE ORIENT

Columbus prepared for his voyage from the Spanish port of Palos. Because he had spent time in Palos when he first came to Spain, he knew people there. This was lucky for Columbus. Being a stranger to the region, he probably wouldn't have found people to sail with him if he hadn't had friends. With the help of several important families in Palos, Columbus found three ships for his voyage and hired skilled sailors to work them. His ships, the *Niña*, the *Pinta*, and the *Santa María*, are among the most famous sailing vessels in history.

By modern standards, the ships were cramped and uncomfortable. Only the ships' captains had berths to themselves. Most of the sailors slept wherever they could find room. With no water for shaving or bathing, they let their beards grow and took cleansing dips in the sea. Cooking was done over an open fire. A metal box set on the deck of the ship served as the fireplace. The food was always the same: hard biscuits that soon became moldy; tough, salty beef; bland cooked beans; and whatever fish the sailors could snag on a line. On long voyages, drinking water was soon covered with green scum, and wine soured. Few modern sailors would work under such conditions. But in Columbus's time, they were very common.

THE NIÑA

After Columbus's flagship, the *Santa María*, was smashed on rocks off of Hispaniola, Columbus commandeered the *Niña*. This ship, shown here, was about 70 feet (21 m) long. This would make the ship only slightly longer than a modern semitrailer, which averages about 65 feet (20 m) long.

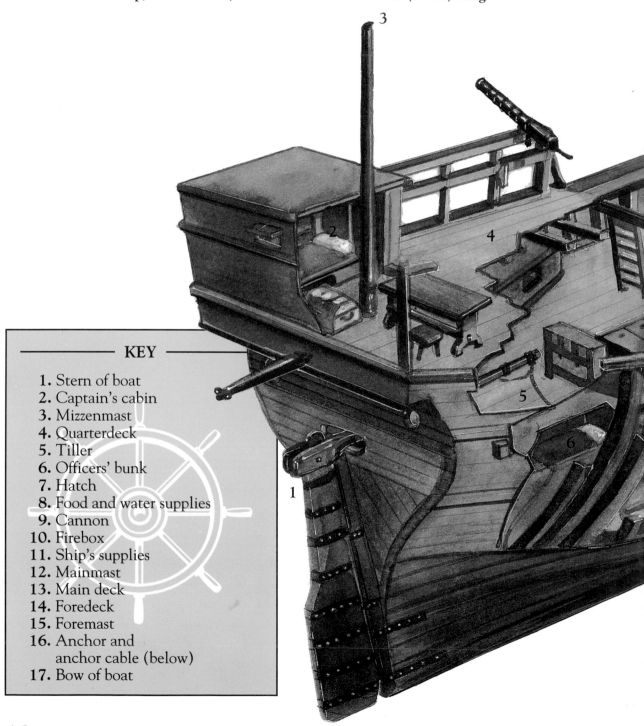

```
KEY
 1. Stern of boat
 2. Captain's cabin
 3. Mizzenmast
 4. Quarterdeck
 5. Tiller
 6. Officers' bunk
 7. Hatch
 8. Food and water supplies
 9. Cannon
10. Firebox
11. Ship's supplies
12. Mainmast
13. Main deck
14. Foredeck
15. Foremast
16. Anchor and
    anchor cable (below)
17. Bow of boat
```

12

15

14

13

17

10

9

7

8

19

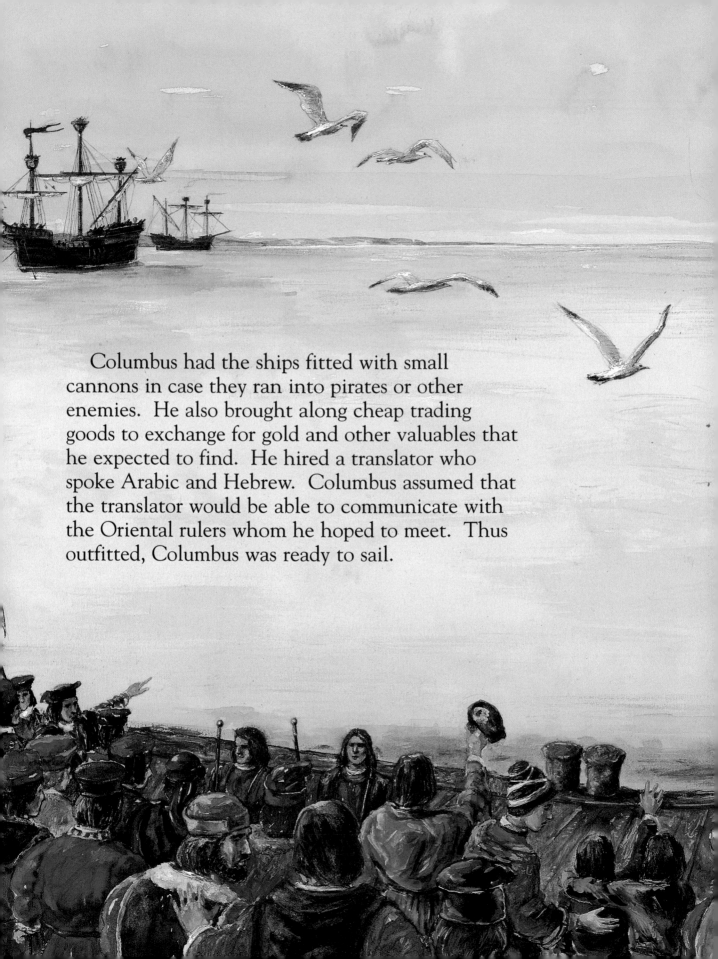

Columbus had the ships fitted with small cannons in case they ran into pirates or other enemies. He also brought along cheap trading goods to exchange for gold and other valuables that he expected to find. He hired a translator who spoke Arabic and Hebrew. Columbus assumed that the translator would be able to communicate with the Oriental rulers whom he hoped to meet. Thus outfitted, Columbus was ready to sail.

On August 3, 1492, the *Niña*, the *Pinta*, and the *Santa María* set out from Spain. Those who watched them from the docks were certain they would never see the ships again.

Columbus and his crew sailed first to the Canary Islands off the coast of Africa. There, they made repairs on the ships and picked up last-minute supplies. Then, on September 6, they pushed off into the unknown Atlantic Ocean.

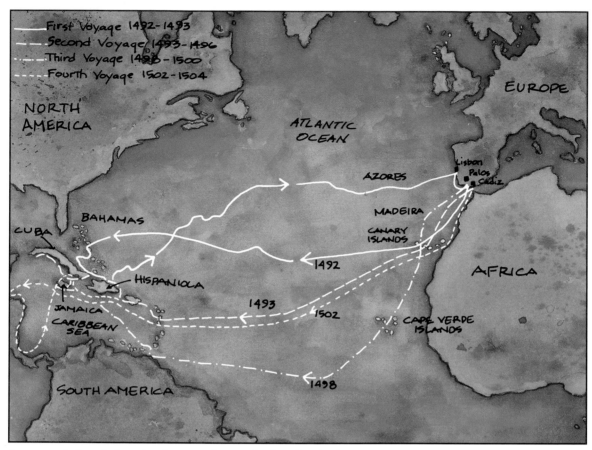

A map of the Atlantic Ocean shows Columbus's four voyages.

Within hours, they were surrounded only by water.

The sailors were nervous from the beginning. The trade winds — strong winds that blow from east to west in regions of the Atlantic — quickly carried the ships away from Africa and Europe.

After ten days of running with the wind, Columbus and the sailors expected to sight land. But no land came into view. The sailors started to mumble about mutiny. Their threats, however, did not stop Columbus. He was sure that they would soon reach the Orient, so he pushed onward.

To find his way across the Atlantic, Columbus had to keep records of three things: the time, the ship's direction, and its speed. Knowing these three things, Columbus could estimate the distance the ships traveled daily.

Keeping track of time was tricky on board Columbus's ships. There were no clocks. Instead, the crew recorded time with an hourglass. To figure out the ship's direction, Columbus used a compass.

Finding the ship's speed was a guessing game. Columbus and his crew watched seaweed and other objects floating on the waves. If the object disappeared from view quickly, they knew they were traveling fast. If the object stayed in sight for a long time, they knew their speed had slowed.

Left: The simple hourglass was the only instrument available for measuring time on ships in the fifteenth, sixteenth, and seventeenth centuries.

Below: History suggests that the Chinese invented the compass. Sailors were using a compass like this one by the twelfth century.

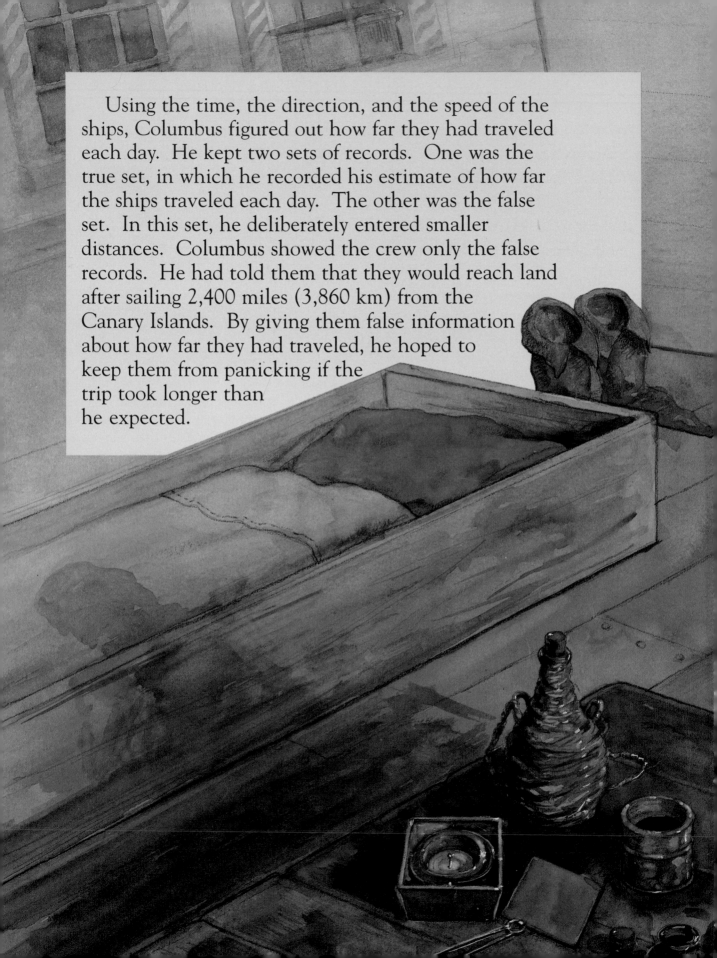

Using the time, the direction, and the speed of the ships, Columbus figured out how far they had traveled each day. He kept two sets of records. One was the true set, in which he recorded his estimate of how far the ships traveled each day. The other was the false set. In this set, he deliberately entered smaller distances. Columbus showed the crew only the false records. He had told them that they would reach land after sailing 2,400 miles (3,860 km) from the Canary Islands. By giving them false information about how far they had traveled, he hoped to keep them from panicking if the trip took longer than he expected.

Nevertheless, the crew continued to be jittery. As September changed into October, their mood turned dangerous. Only Columbus's iron will and strong action by the other captains prevented the sailors from rising up in rebellion.

Luckily for Columbus, the ships were not far from land. The sailors noticed great flocks of birds flying southwest. Columbus changed course to follow them. Within a few days, the sailors were picking up pieces of driftwood and even broken branches floating by on the waves. Now, no one doubted Columbus's wisdom. Land was certainly in easy reach.

On the night of October 12, 1492, a sailor on the *Pinta* spotted the gleam of white cliffs in the moonlight. "Land! Land!" the sailor called out joyfully. Early in the morning, the men went ashore. They had landed on a small island in what are now called the Bahamas. Columbus named the island San Salvador and claimed it for Spain.

It was not long before several naked, golden-skinned people approached the Spanish sailors. Since Columbus was sure that he had reached the Indies — islands off the coast of Asia — he called these people Indians. The Indians who lived on this tiny island were members of a group now known as the Arawak. They lived simply, raising corn and yams for food. They wove their few clothes from cotton that they grew, and they made simple clay pots for cooking and hauling water. They slept on hammocks, woven beds they hung between two trees. European sailors adopted this comfortable style of bedding for long ocean voyages.

Columbus soon realized that his translator could be of no help on this island. To communicate, then, the Indians and the sailors relied on simple gestures.

The Indians were not at all shy. They showed the sailors their villages and were happy to trade everything they had for the glass beads and silver bells Columbus had brought.

The sailors spent two days exploring San Salvador. They marveled at the tall trees and the lush, green plants that covered most of the island. They picked sweet-smelling flowers that grew on vines and noted the colorful tropical birds flitting about the forest. Columbus decided the island was one of the most beautiful places he had ever visited.

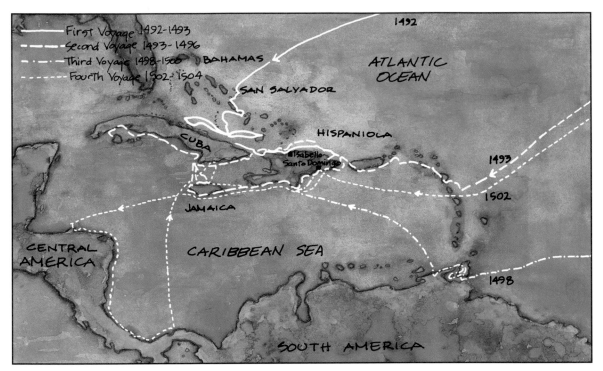

Columbus's travels carried him to many places throughout the Caribbean Sea.

But scenery was not Columbus's main interest. He wanted to make his way to Japan or China, to the courts of the Oriental rulers who controlled the gold, spices, and jewels. Noting that some of the Indians wore small gold rings in their noses, Columbus asked where the gold came from. The Indians pointed toward the west.

With that, Columbus decided to sail on. He took six Indians with him to act as guides. The three ships sailed in and out of the tiny Bahama Islands, but nowhere did they find gold. About ten days later, Columbus and his crew went ashore on a large island today known as Cuba. The Indians on that island indicated that gold could be found at "Cubanacan," and pointed toward the center of the island. When Columbus heard the name, he became excited. He thought the Indians were referring to Kublai Khan, China's famous ruler. He sent an exploring party to find the emperor's court, but the men returned disappointed. All they had found was a large Indian village, but no Kublai Khan and no gold. Still convinced that he had landed on Asian shores, Columbus sailed on.

Through November, Columbus and crew explored Cuba's coast. In December, they traveled to another large island that Columbus named Hispaniola. The Indians there swam out to the ships to greet them. These people had plenty of gold that they eagerly traded for trinkets that the Europeans offered. Indian leaders met with Columbus, and they entertained each other in style. The Indians gave Columbus gifts of gold jewelry. Columbus honored the Indians with a booming twenty-one-gun salute.

Some of the native people that Columbus met in his travels were friendly toward the Europeans. Often, it was only after much abuse that these people became hostile.

Disaster struck on Christmas Day. The *Santa María* ran aground on a coral reef just off the coast of Hispaniola. With huge gashes in its hull, the ship could not be repaired. Columbus ordered the crew to salvage any supplies they could and to abandon ship.

This event would have left most people in despair, but Columbus rejoiced. He was convinced that the grounding of the *Santa María* was a sign from God. He believed it meant that the sailors were to start a colony on Hispaniola. About twenty men volunteered to stay behind. Before Columbus left, they began building a fort with timbers from the

wreck of the *Santa María*. Columbus himself decided to return to Spain. With a cannon salute to the men remaining on Hispaniola, Columbus and the rest of the crew set sail in January. Columbus also took aboard several Indians to prove that he had reached other lands.

On March 15, 1493, Columbus reached Spain. He was sent for by King Ferdinand and Queen Isabella, who honored him with gifts, titles, and their highest praise. Suddenly, Columbus was the most famous man in all of Europe.

Columbus and his crew return to Spain in glory at the end of the first voyage.

4

FROM FAME TO FAILURE

Columbus, however, was not a man to sit idly, enjoying this glory. Instead, he began to prepare for a second voyage. This expedition was a colonizing venture as well as a voyage of exploration. Columbus was in charge of a fleet of seventeen ships that carried 1,500 people. Among the people were soldiers, adventurers, men looking to make their fortunes from gold, and priests sent to convert the Indians to Christianity. They brought horses and other livestock and enough food to last six months. On September 25, 1493, the ships pulled out of the Spanish harbor of Cadiz, their colorful flags flying in the breeze.

Columbus's ships crossed the Atlantic in record time. On November 3, the crew first sighted land. They explored a number of islands in the southern Caribbean. Then, Columbus landed on Hispaniola, where he had left his sailors to settle the year before. But no one answered his greeting cannon shot. All the men had been killed. Apparently, these colonists had behaved brutally, forcing the Indians to work for them and demanding large quantities of gold from them. In the end, the Indians had wiped out the settlement.

Columbus sailed on and founded another settlement on Hispaniola. He named the new town Isabella after the Spanish queen. He put the colonists to work building the town, sent an exploring party into the interior to look for gold, and then sailed off in search of the court of the emperor of China.

Opposite: Lush tropical islands bordered by warm, sandy beaches greeted Columbus throughout his travels in the Caribbean Sea.

Columbus was known as a cruel governor in the New World colonies that he founded. Those who rebelled against him — whether native or colonist — were dealt with harshly.

Weaving in and out of the Caribbean islands, Columbus looked for signs of Chinese culture. Nowhere did he find the tile-roofed pagodas or the graceful arched bridges he thought he would find. Still, he remained certain that the large island of Cuba, on which he had landed during his first voyage, was the mainland of Asia. He spent a month sailing along the island's coast.

By mid-June 1494, he had almost run out of food, and his ships needed repair. He made the men sign a paper stating that they had reached the Asian coast and threatened to punish anyone who claimed otherwise. Then he turned the ships around and headed back to Hispaniola.

The journey back to the colony was rough. Columbus became ill near the end of the trip and had to be carried ashore when they reached Isabella. The colony itself was also falling apart. Many of the men were sick from tropical diseases. Some had died. Food supplies were low because the Spanish had not planted crops. Instead they demanded that the Indians feed them. But the Indians, tired of harsh treatment by the Spaniards, were in no mood to be generous. They banded together against the intruders.

Columbus only made the situation worse. Once he had recovered from his illness, he rounded up thousands of Indians and sent them to Spain. There they were sold as slaves. He demanded that the Indians that remained bring him a monthly tribute of gold. If they failed to do this, they were killed. Columbus was just as harsh with the Spanish colonists who disobeyed him. He had them executed as well.

Eventually, word of Columbus's cruelty reached

Columbus returned to Hispaniola in 1493 to find that Indians had wiped out the colonists. In Columbus's absence, the Europeans had abused the natives. Sadly, Columbus did little to improve the situation.

The Caribbean Sea, where Columbus did much of his exploring, is known for hurricanes. As seen here, such fierce storms were a danger to exploration.

Ferdinand and Isabella. Colonists returning to Spain complained to the king and queen about Columbus. In March 1496, Columbus decided to go back to Spain. He wanted to give the king and queen his side of the story.

Columbus's return to Spain in the summer of 1496 was hardly impressive. As his ship docked, fifty half-starved Spanish colonists and a few naked Indians disembarked from it. The gold, the spices, the silks, the wealth of the Orient were nowhere to be seen. Even so, Columbus was able to convince Ferdinand and Isabella that the Indies would yield riches. They granted him eight ships to make yet another voyage.

In May 1498, Columbus set sail across the Atlantic for the third time. This time he sailed in a more southward direction and first sighted land along the coast of South America. Because he did not expect to find a continent, Columbus assumed that the landmass was a large island. He claimed it for Spain. After exploring the coastal region for a month, he sailed to Hispaniola to check on the Spanish colony.

Before Columbus had returned to Spain in 1496, a hurricane had destroyed the colony at Isabella. At once, the Spaniards had begun work on a new town. The town, called Santo Domingo, was complete before Columbus returned in August 1498.

In the new colony, Columbus found many of the same problems that plagued the old colony. The colonists had rebelled against Columbus's brother Bartholomew, who governed Santo Domingo while Columbus was in Spain. They weren't any happier when Columbus himself returned. Life was more difficult than the colonists had expected. And they weren't gaining any of the riches they had left their homeland for. So many colonists returned home in disgust that Ferdinand and Isabella decided to send a trusted court adviser, Francisco de Bobadilla, to investigate.

When word of trouble in the colonies reached Spain, Francisco de Bobadilla was sent to investigate. He was displeased enough with what he saw to have Christopher and Bartholomew Columbus arrested.

The first thing Bobadilla saw when he landed at Santo Domingo was seven Spanish colonists hanging from the gallows. These men had rebelled against Columbus, and his brothers Bartholomew and Diego had them executed.

This manner of handling criminals did not please Bobadilla. He threw Columbus and his brothers in jail and began governing the colony himself. In no time, he had collected a thick file of complaints against Columbus. He decided to send the explorer back to Spain for trial. Chained like a common criminal, Columbus was hustled on board a ship. In October 1500, the ship landed in Spain, and Columbus was led down the gangway in shame.

Ferdinand and Isabella felt bad when they saw Columbus in chains. They ordered him released and then pardoned him for any errors he might have made in governing Hispaniola. But they did not restore his power over the colony. By this time, the rulers of Spain realized that Columbus was as skillful a navigator as they could ever hope to find. As a governor, however, he was a complete failure.

Columbus returned again and again to the royal court begging to be sent on another voyage. He wanted to find more lands to colonize and to prove that his western route indeed led to the Orient. In March 1502, Columbus sailed from Spain on his fourth voyage.

Columbus spent most of this final voyage exploring the eastern coast of the region that is today known as Central America. Sailing was slow and dangerous. The weather was horrible. Heavy rains fell for months at a time. Columbus had no luck finding a passageway through the landmass to the Indian Ocean, which he was sure was very close by. He did, however, find Indians who would trade their gold. But when Columbus and crew tried to build a trading colony in the area, the Indians gathered to attack them. The explorers barely escaped with their lives.

After a year of sailing, Columbus's ships had become riddled with worms. The ships were leaking badly when the crew left Central America. Columbus landed on the island now called Jamaica. He hauled the ships ashore and sent some of his men in a canoe to Santo Domingo. There they were to find a new ship to take them back to Spain. The new governor of Santo Domingo gloated over Columbus's bad luck. He took his time in sending a ship to Jamaica. Columbus waited for more than a year before he could set sail for Spain.

Columbus finally made it back to Spain in November 1504. He never went to sea again. Although he kept insisting he had found his way to the Orient, people only laughed at him. He died on May 19, 1506, a lonely, angry man.

5

THE CONTROVERSY OVER COLUMBUS

Was Christopher Columbus a success or a failure? Was he a hero or a villain? Was he even who people think he was? Over the years, various people have claimed that Columbus was not Italian, but Spanish, Portuguese, Greek, English, Irish, Norwegian, or Jewish. The fact is that no one can say with certainty what his ancestry was.

The same kinds of controversies surround his accomplishments. Few people today claim that Columbus "discovered" the Americas. After all, millions of people already lived on these continents when Columbus traveled across the Atlantic. Most people even agree that Columbus was not the first European to land on the Americas or the islands off their shores. The Phoenicians may have sailed to these lands in ancient times. And the Vikings landed on the coast of what is today Canada five hundred years before Columbus made it to the Caribbean. Some people even think that Portuguese sailors landed on the island now known as Puerto Rico eight years before Columbus set sail on his first voyage.

Despite these problems, many people agree that Christopher Columbus is an important figure. He may not have been the first European to sail to the Americas. But his voyage launched a wave of settlement that, for better or worse, changed the history of the world.

Opposite: Christopher Columbus, navigator and explorer. Without a doubt, he changed people's ideas about the world.

THE LEGACY OF COLUMBUS

Christopher Columbus started an exchange of cultures that changed life in the Old World of Europe, Africa, and Asia, as well as the New World of the Americas. Some of the changes were not good. Diseases carried across the ocean, for example, killed millions of people on both sides of it. But other changes were more positive. For one, the Indians introduced the Europeans to new foods, such as the potato and the yam. These foods became staples in the diets of many European and African people. Europeans brought horses to the New World, forever changing the life-style of many Indian groups.

Although he died a forgotten man, Columbus is one of history's most famous figures. In the United States, cities such as Columbus, Ohio; Columbia, South Carolina; and the nation's capital, the District of Columbia, are named for him. The Canadian province of British Columbia is named for him. The South American nation of Colombia is also named for Columbus, and several South American cities are named Colón, which is Spanish for "Columbus." Even in Sri Lanka, an island to the south of India, the capital city, Colombo, honors the explorer.

Columbus ushered in the modern world, with its destructiveness as well as its dreams, its creativity as well as its conflicts. For these things, Columbus will be remembered for centuries to come.

CHRONOLOGY

1451 Christopher Columbus is born in Genoa, Italy.

1476 Columbus is shipwrecked off the coast of Portugal, swims to shore, and spends the next eight years of his life sailing for the Portuguese.

1484 Columbus proposes his idea of sailing west to the Orient to King John II of Portugal. The Portuguese king rejects the idea.

1486 Columbus first presents his proposal to King Ferdinand and Queen Isabella of Spain and is rejected.

1492 Ferdinand and Isabella are convinced to sponsor Columbus.
August — Columbus sets sail across the Atlantic from Palos.
October — Columbus lands on the islands that are today called the Bahamas.
December — Columbus establishes the first European colony on Hispaniola.

1493 **March** — Columbus returns to Spain and receives the highest honors from King Ferdinand and Queen Isabella.
September — Columbus sets off on his second voyage across the Atlantic Ocean.

1494 **January** — After finding his first colony on Hispaniola destroyed, Columbus starts a second colony known as Isabella.

1495 The colony of Isabella is destroyed in a hurricane.

1496 Columbus's brother Bartholomew starts a new colony, named Santo Domingo, on Hispaniola. Columbus returns to Spain.

1498 **May** — Columbus sails from Spain on his third voyage.
August — Columbus lands on the continent of South America and claims it for Spain.

1500 Columbus is accused of mismanaging the colony of Santo Domingo and is sent back to Spain in chains.
December — Ferdinand and Isabella pardon Columbus.

1502 Columbus sets sail on his fourth voyage. He explores the coast of Central America.

1503-1504 Columbus spends more than a year marooned on Jamaica.

1504 Columbus returns to Spain.

1506 Columbus dies in Valladolid, Spain.

GLOSSARY

Arawak: A tribe of Indians that lived in the Caribbean. The first natives of the New World to greet Columbus, they were enslaved and almost wiped out by the Spanish colonists.

barter: To swap or trade one thing for something else.

berth: A built-in bed or bunk in a ship for members of the crew to sleep in.

caravan: A group of merchants traveling together for greater safety. Some caravans crossed thousands of miles to bring silk and spices from the Orient back to Europe.

compass: A Chinese invention for finding direction. A compass contains a small magnet that always points north.

hereditary: Passed along from parent to child. Columbus demanded that he be made governor of any lands he discovered. He also asked that the position be a hereditary one so that it would pass to his descendants.

hourglass: A simple timekeeping instrument. An hourglass is a glass container divided into two compartments that are connected by a narrow neck. Time is measured as a set amount of sand, water, or other material flows from the upper compartment into the lower.

hurricane: A fierce tropical storm known for powerful, destructive winds. Hurricanes can have winds as strong as 180 miles (290 km) per hour and are often accompanied by heavy rain, thunder, and lightning.

Indian: A native of India or the East Indies; also, a native of the New World. Since Columbus thought that he had reached India, he called the native Americans he met "Indians."

Kublai Khan (1215-94): The Mongol emperor of China who was visited by Marco Polo.

marooned: To be shipwrecked or abandoned. On his last voyage, Columbus and his men were marooned on an island for over a year.

Moors: Descendants of the Muslims who had invaded Spain in the eighth century and remained in power until the seventeenth century.

Muslim: A follower of Islam, one of the world's major religions.

mutiny: A rebellion in which soldiers, sailors, or other subordinates refuse to obey their leader's orders and may even attempt to overthrow the leader.

New World: The Western Hemisphere — North, Central, and South America.

Old World: The Eastern Hemisphere — including Europe, Africa, and Asia.

Orient: Literally "the East." This region includes China, Japan, India, and Indonesia, which includes islands that used to be known as the Spice Islands.

BOOKS TO READ

The following books will tell you more about Christopher Columbus, other explorers, and related topics.

Christopher Columbus, Who Sailed On!
Dorothy F. Richards (Child's World)
Explorers of America: Columbus.
Dan Zadra (Pelican)
Great Adventures That Changed Our World. (Reader's Digest Association)
The Great Explorers. Piers Pennington (Facts on File)
The Log of Christopher Columbus's First Voyage to America: In the

Year 1492, As Copied Out in Brief by Bartholomew Las Casas. (Shoe String)
Meet Christopher Columbus.
James T. DeKay (Random House)
The Ships of Columbus. (Capstone Press)
The Value of Curiosity: The Story of Christopher Columbus.
Spencer Johnson (Oak Tree)

PLACES TO WRITE

The following organizations can provide you with more information about Christopher Columbus, as well as other explorers and explorations. When you write to them, be sure to tell them exactly what you would like to know and include your name, complete address, and age. You should also enclose a self-addressed, stamped envelope for a reply.

Columbus: Countdown 1992
166-25 Powells Cove Boulevard
Beechhurst, New York 11357

American Geographical Society Collection
Golda Meir Library
University of Wisconsin-Milwaukee
P.O. Box 604
Milwaukee, Wisconsin 53201

Discovery Five Hundred
P.O. Box 1492
Columbus, New Jersey 08022

Christopher Columbus Quincentenary Jubilee Commission
1801 F Street NW
Washington, D.C. 20006

INDEX